This Book Belongs To:

____

____

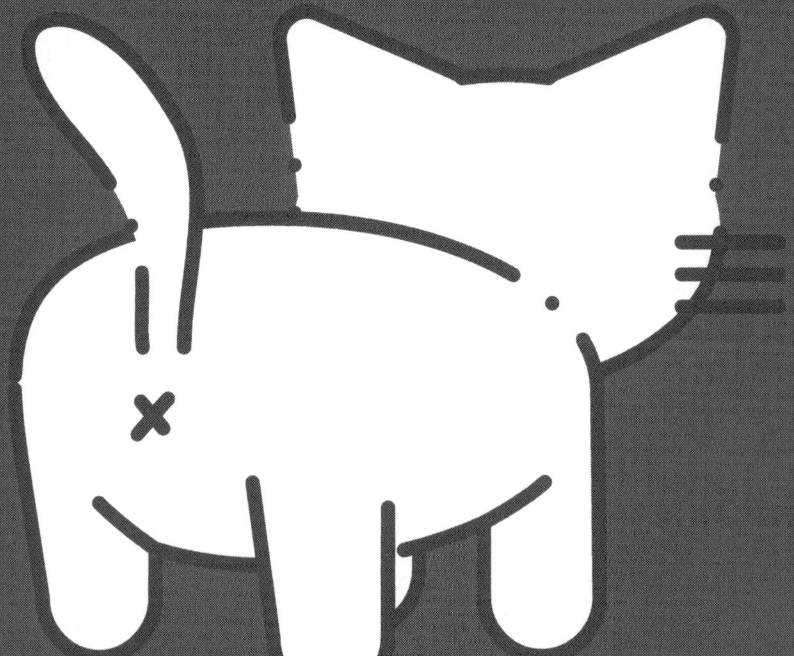

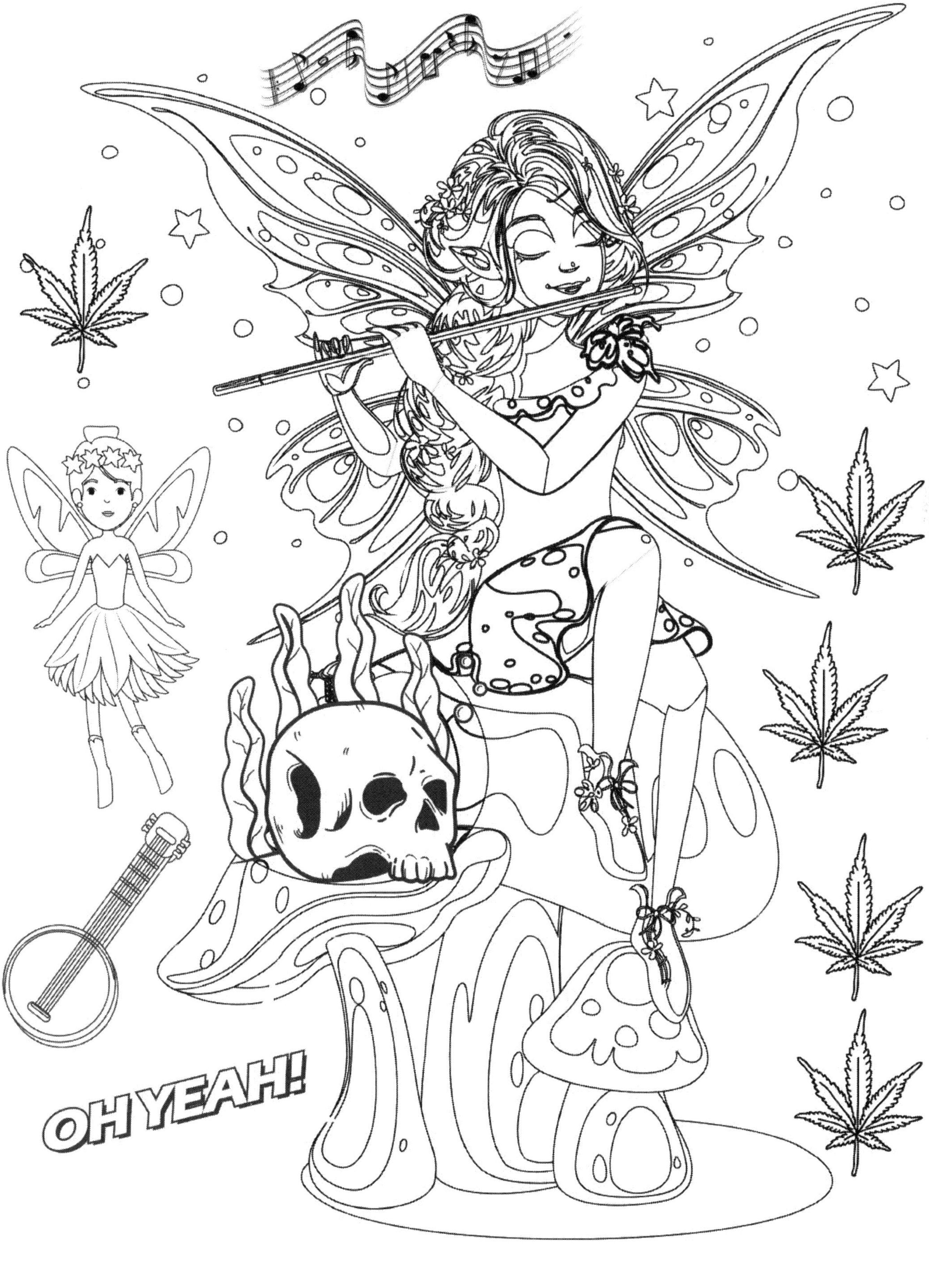
OH YEAH!

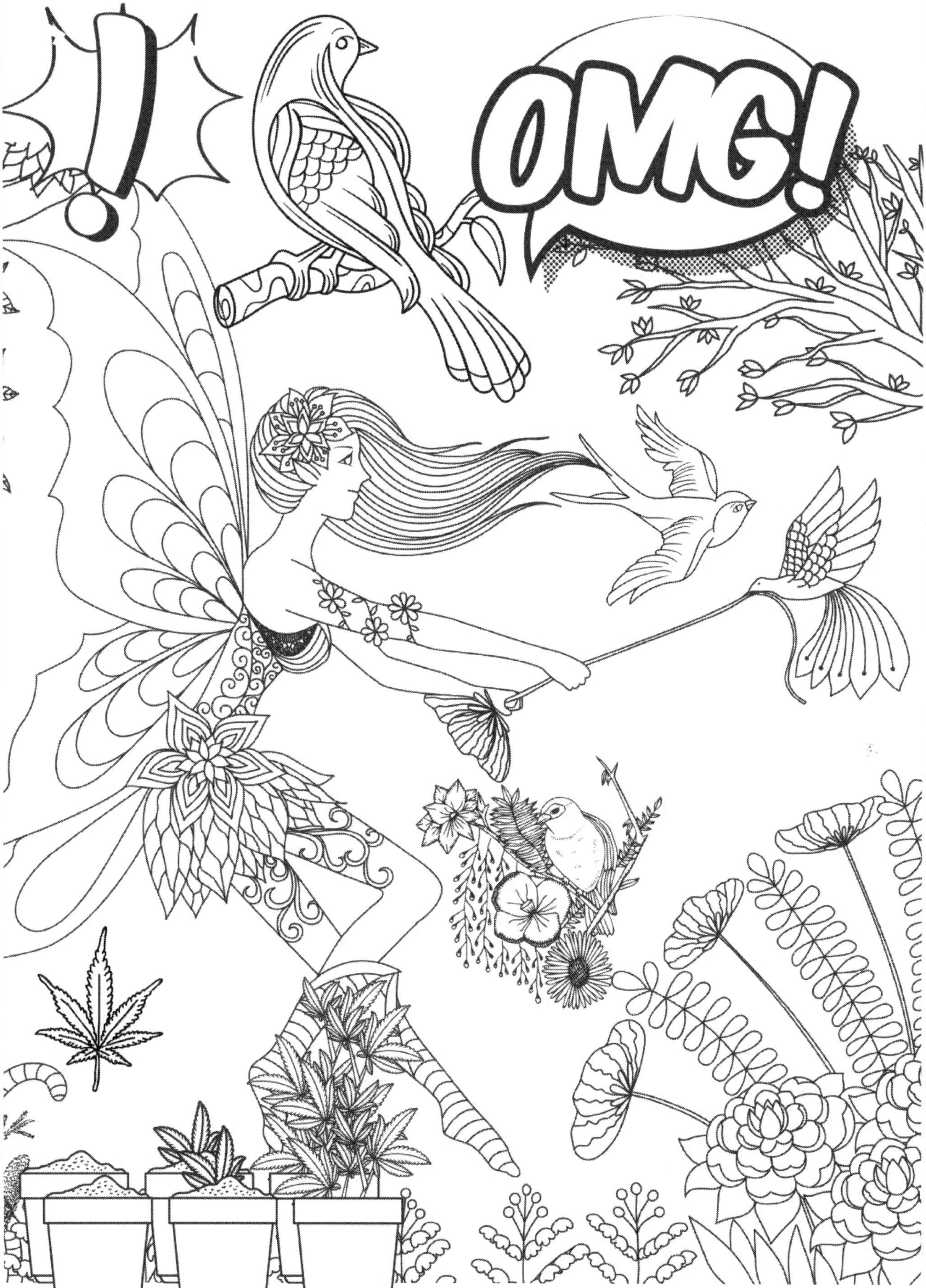
!
OMG!

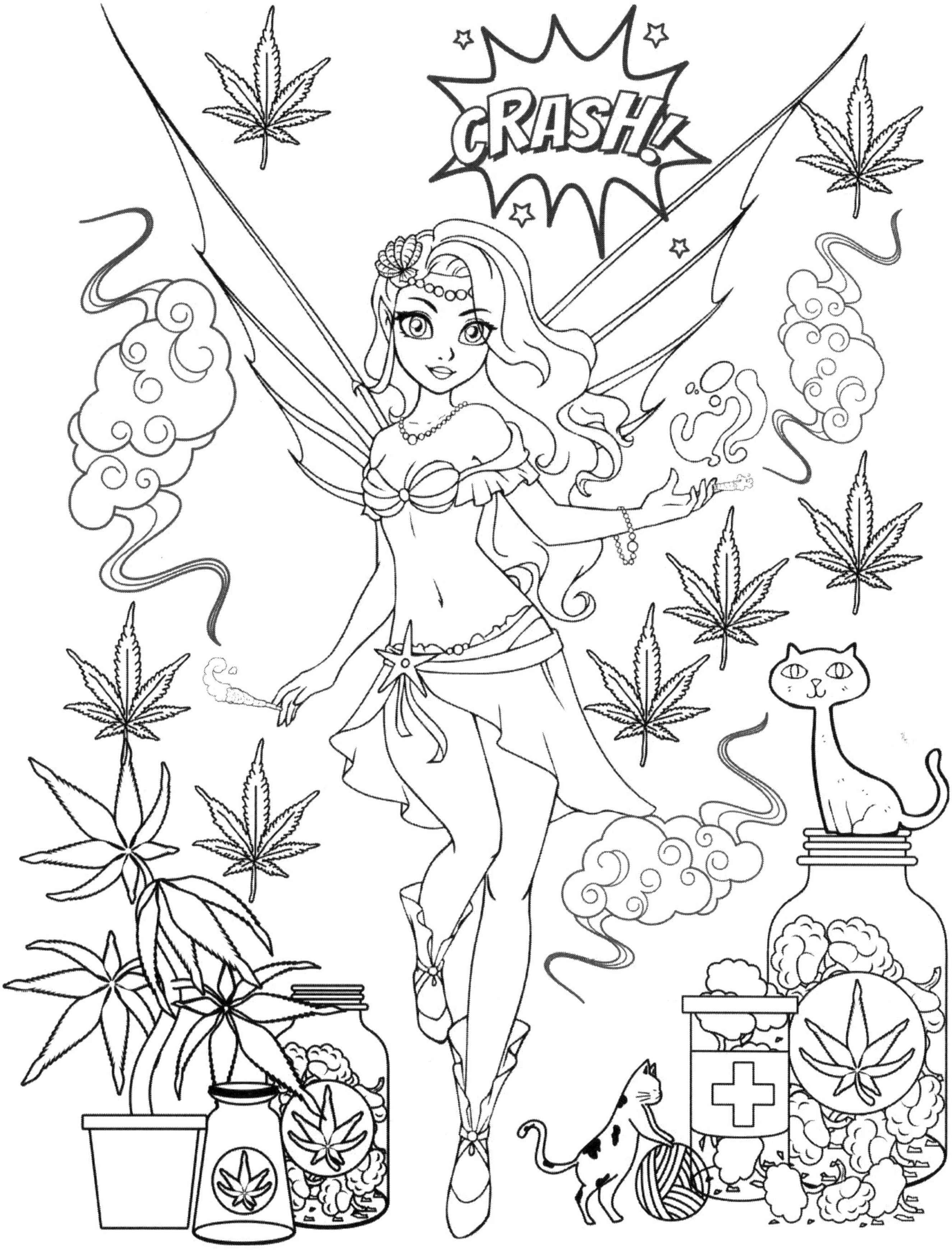
CRASH!

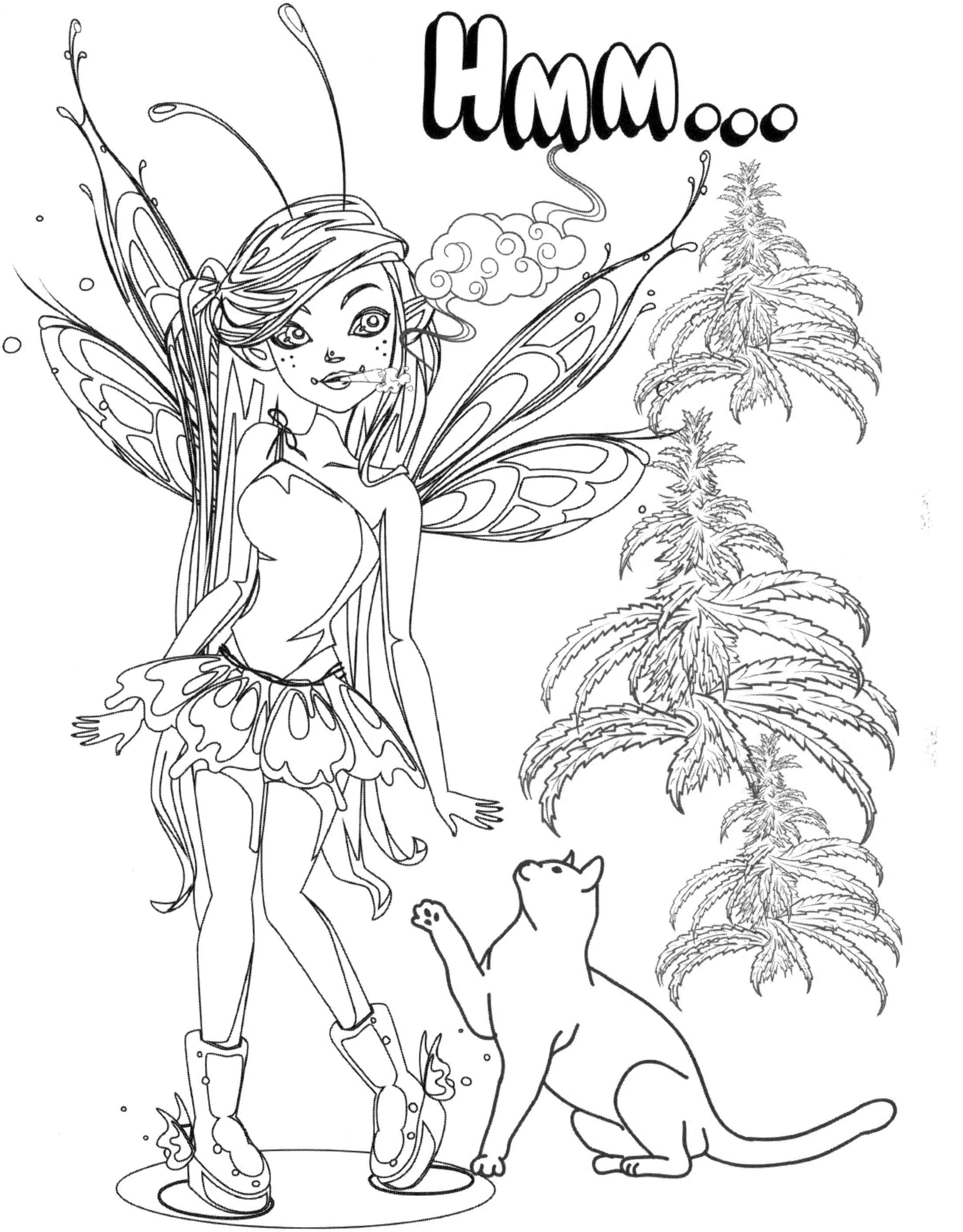
Hmm...

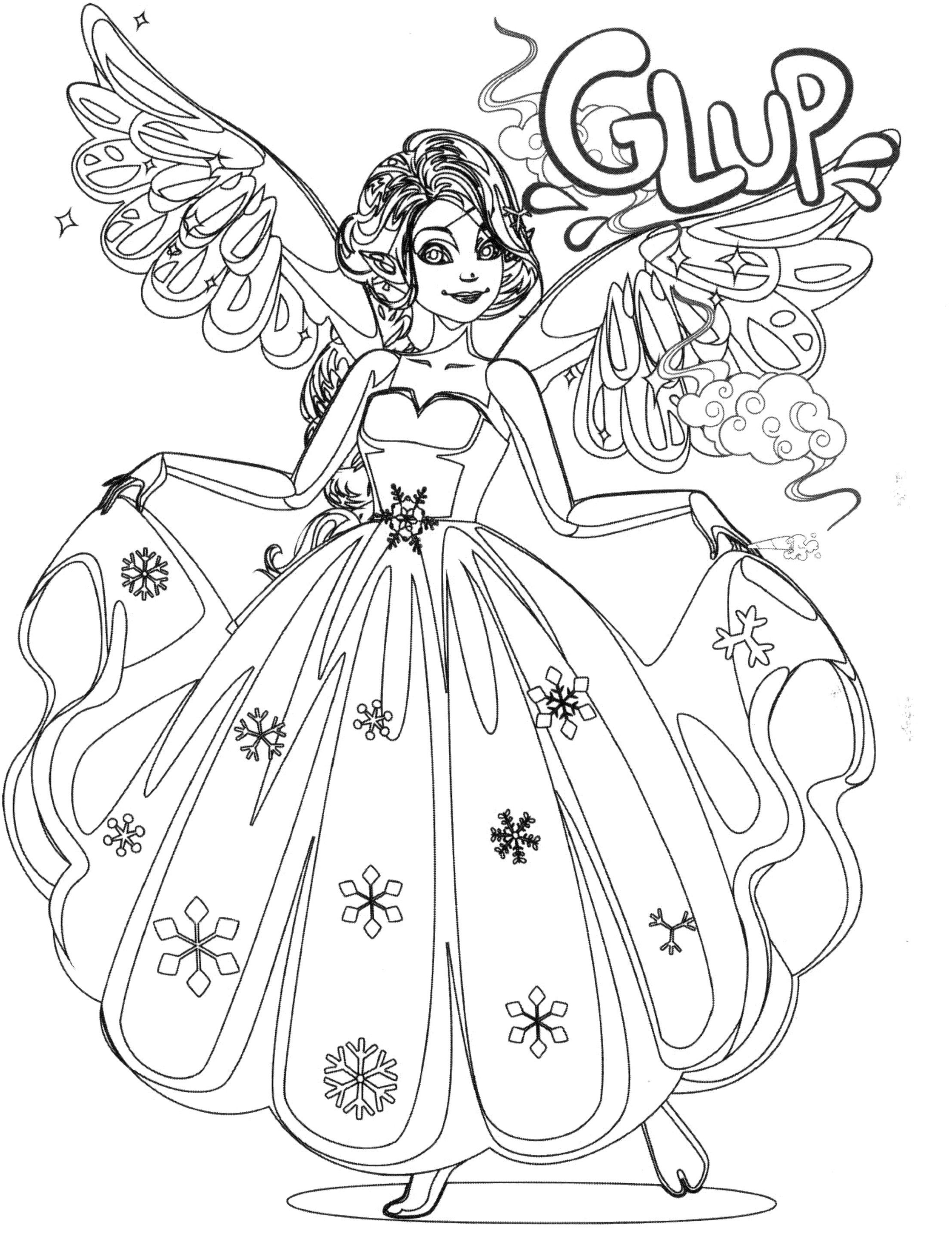
GLUP

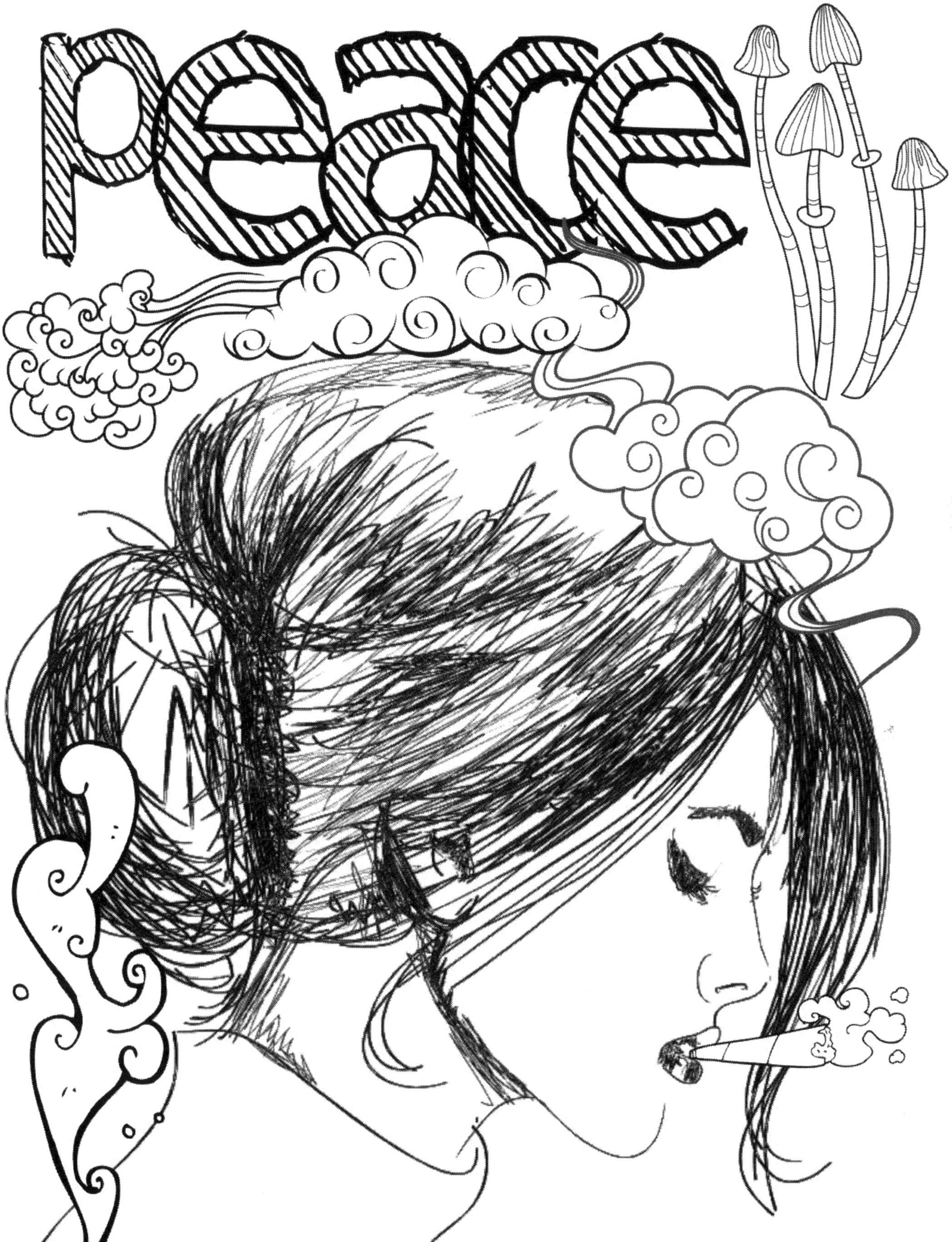
peace

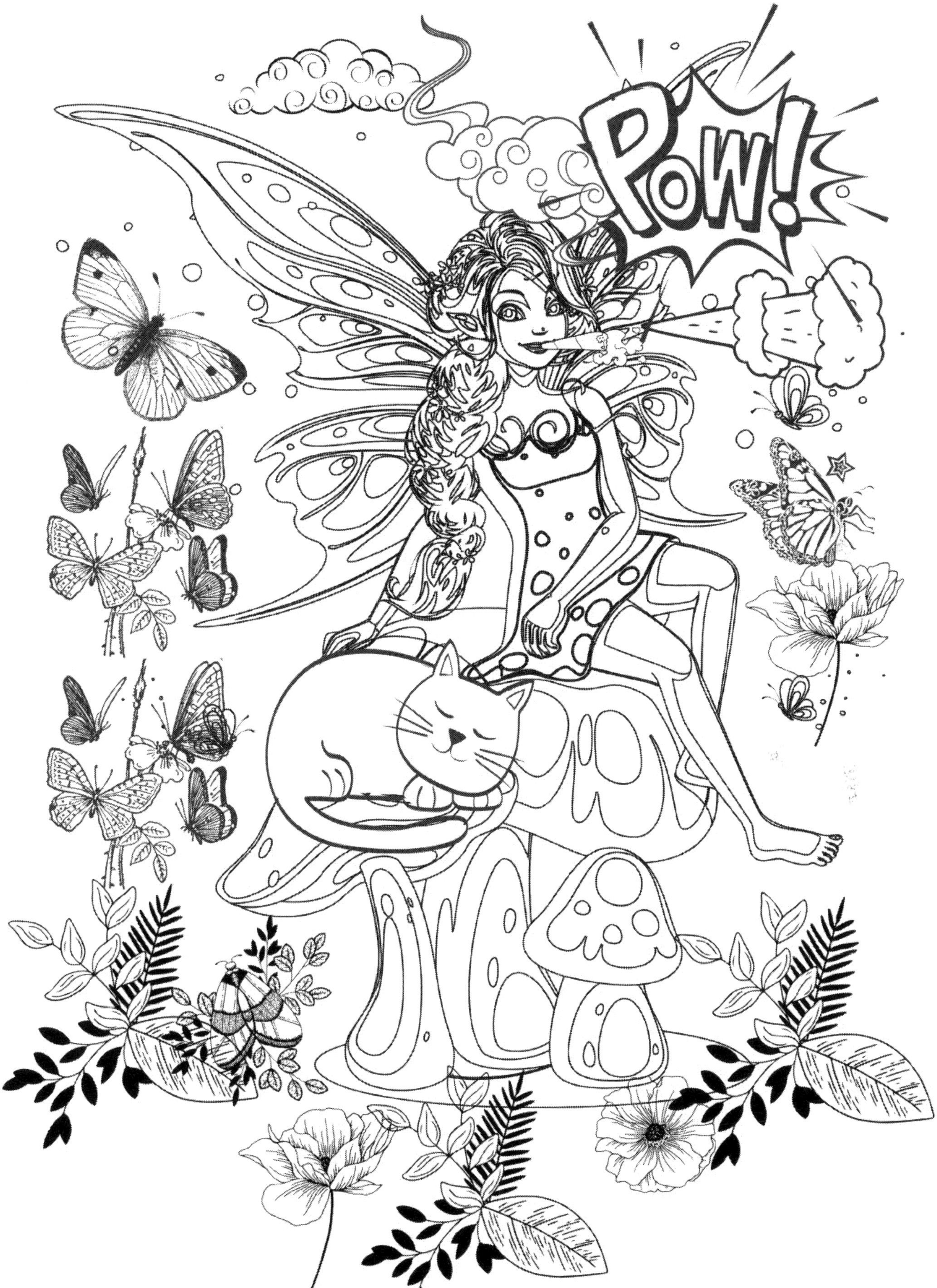
POW!

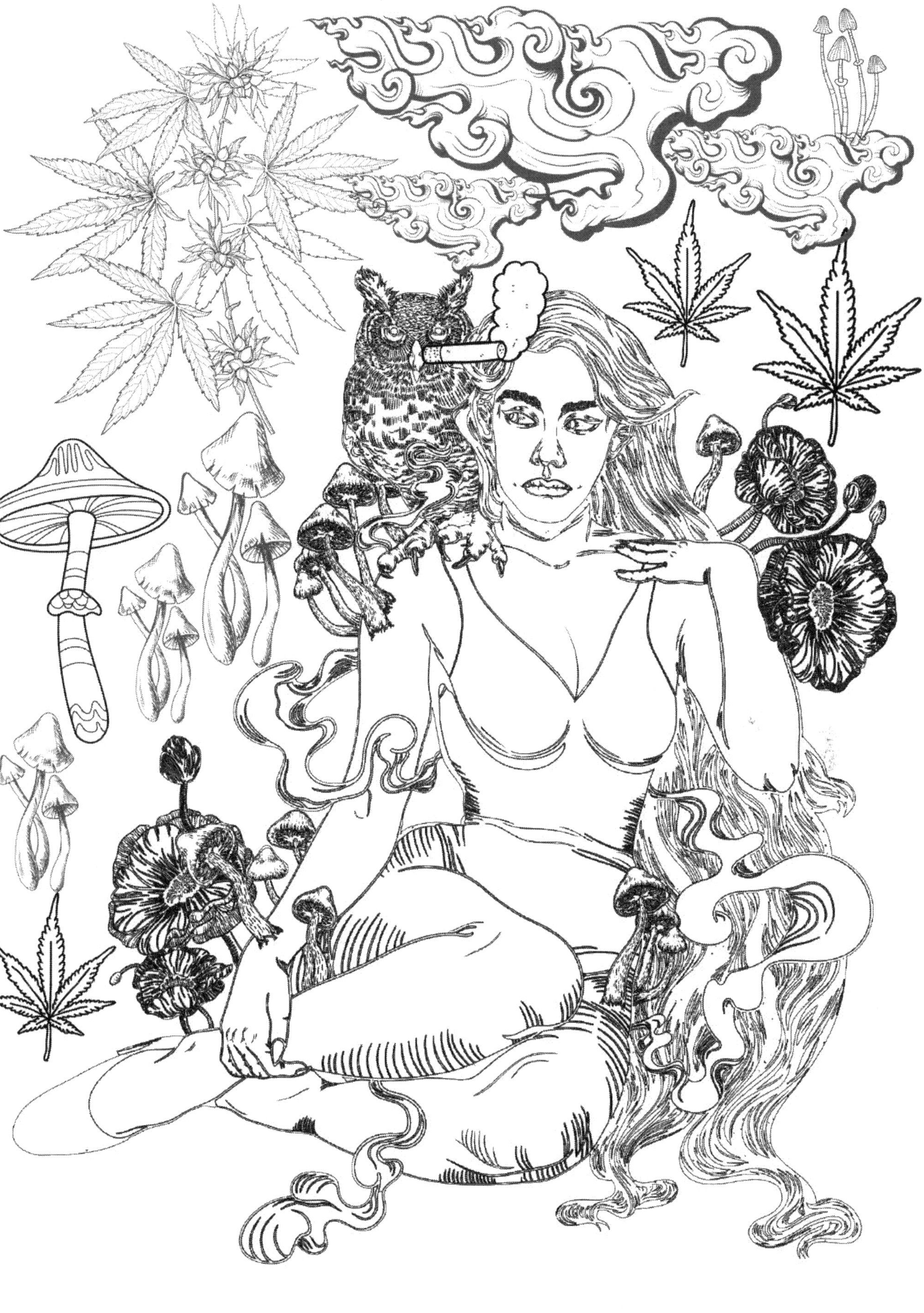

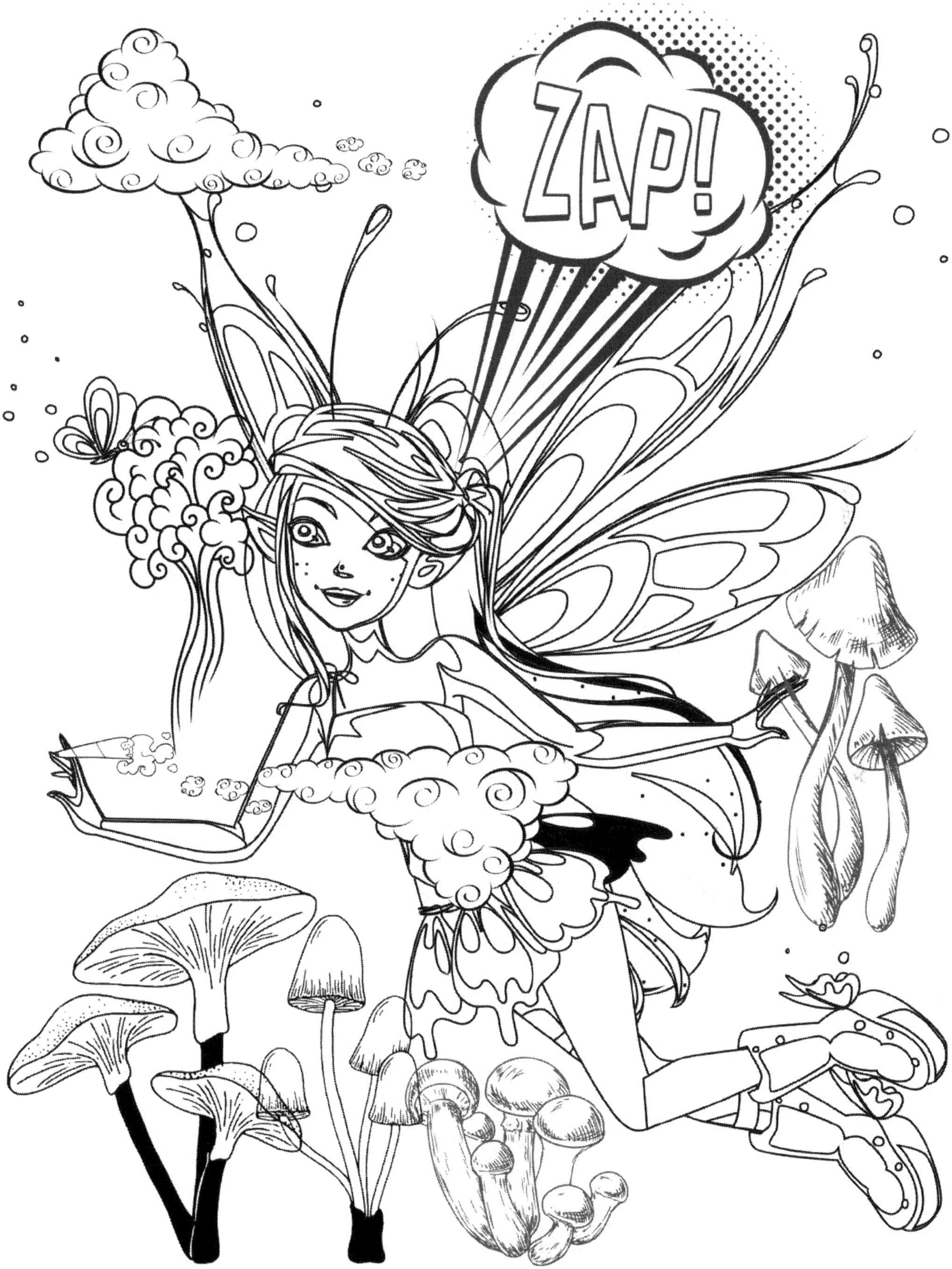
ZAP!

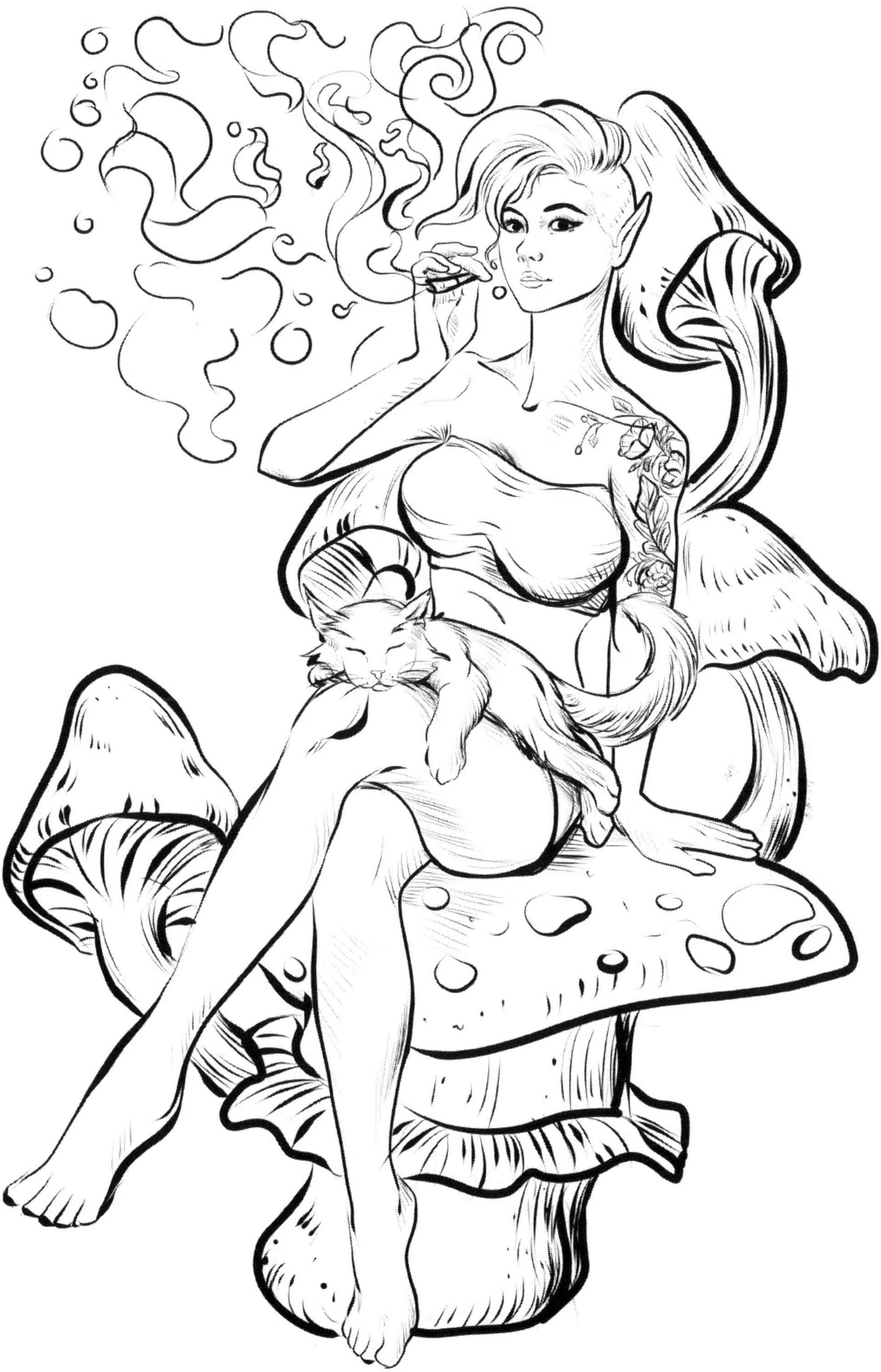

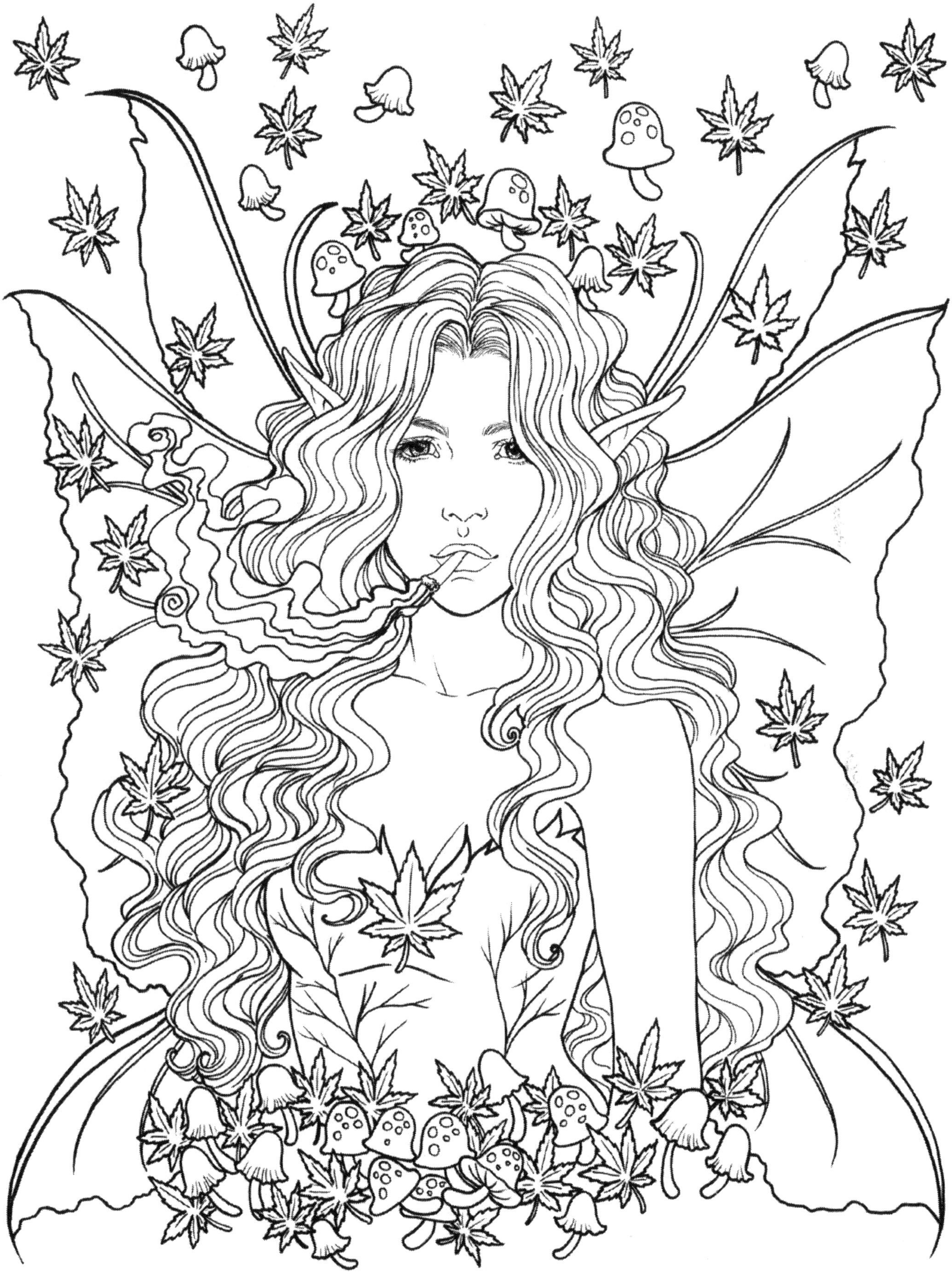

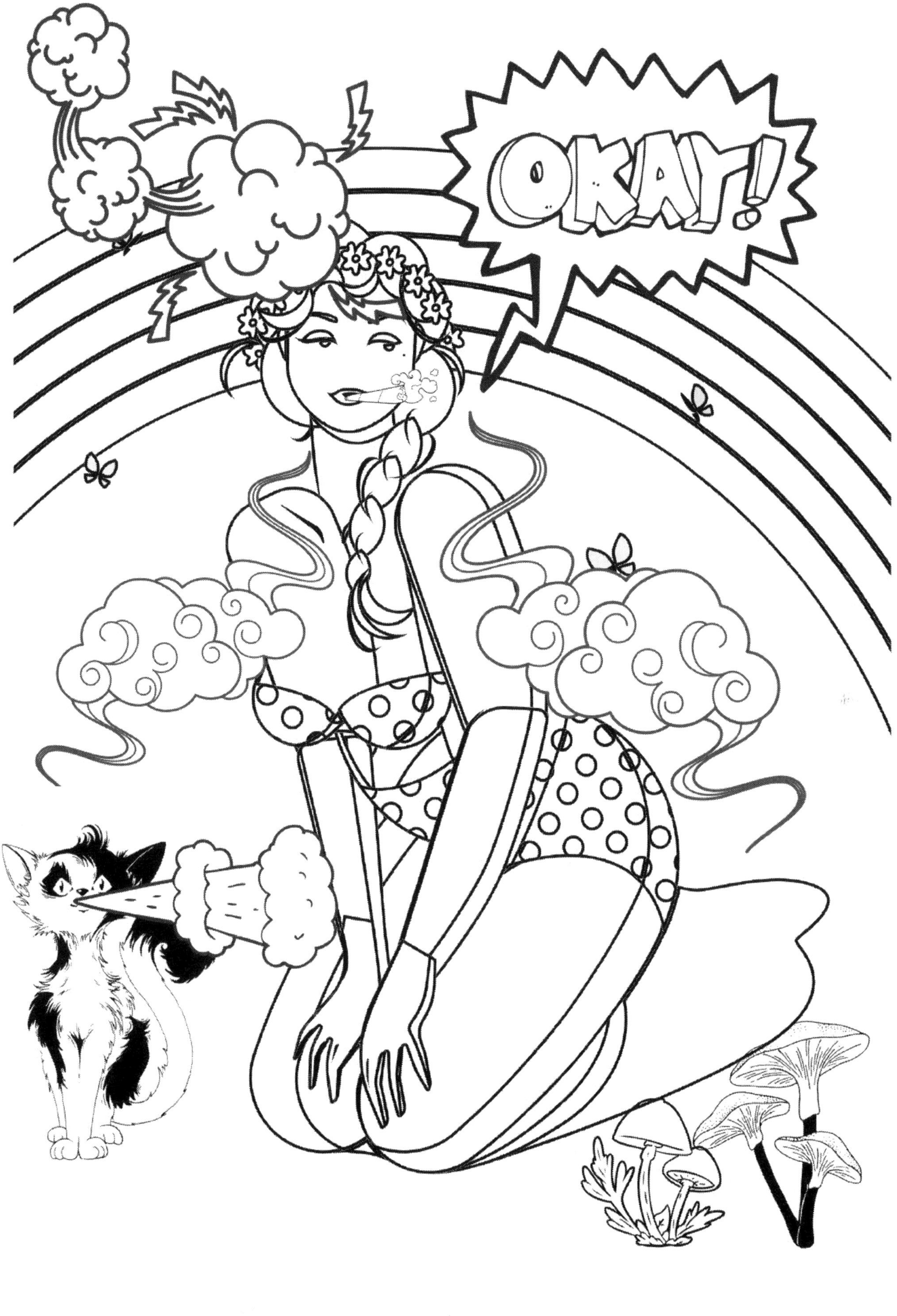
OKAY!

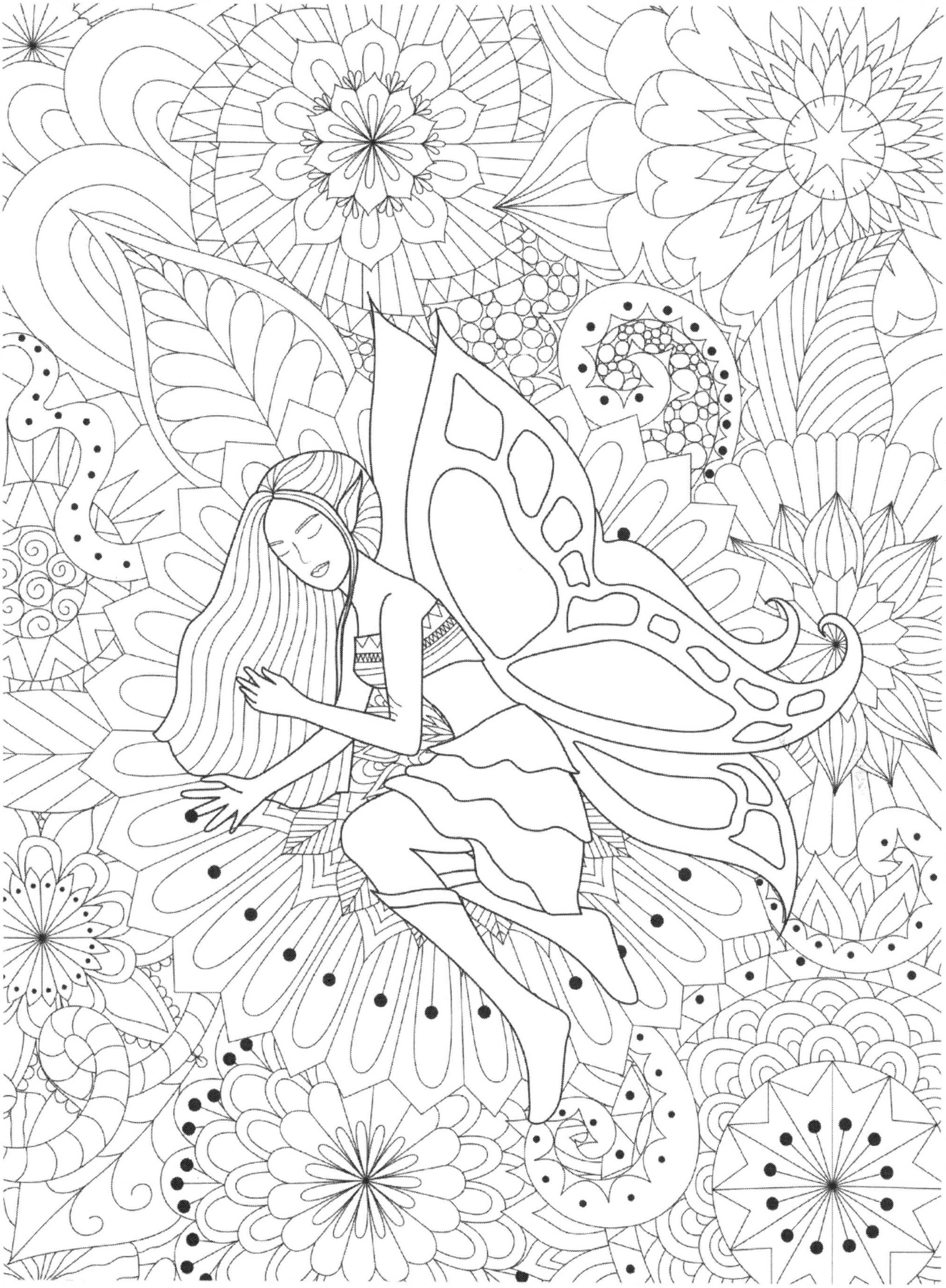

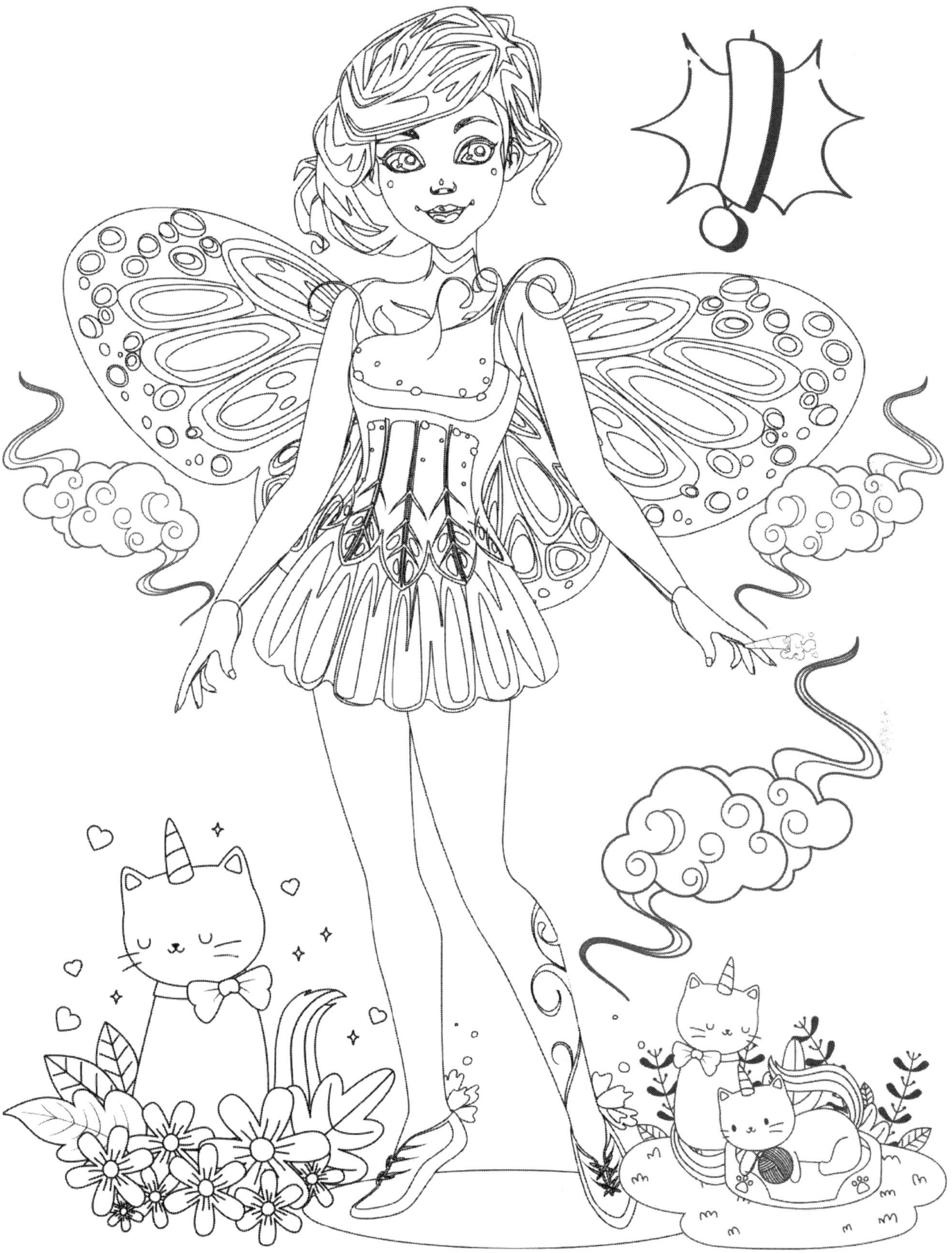

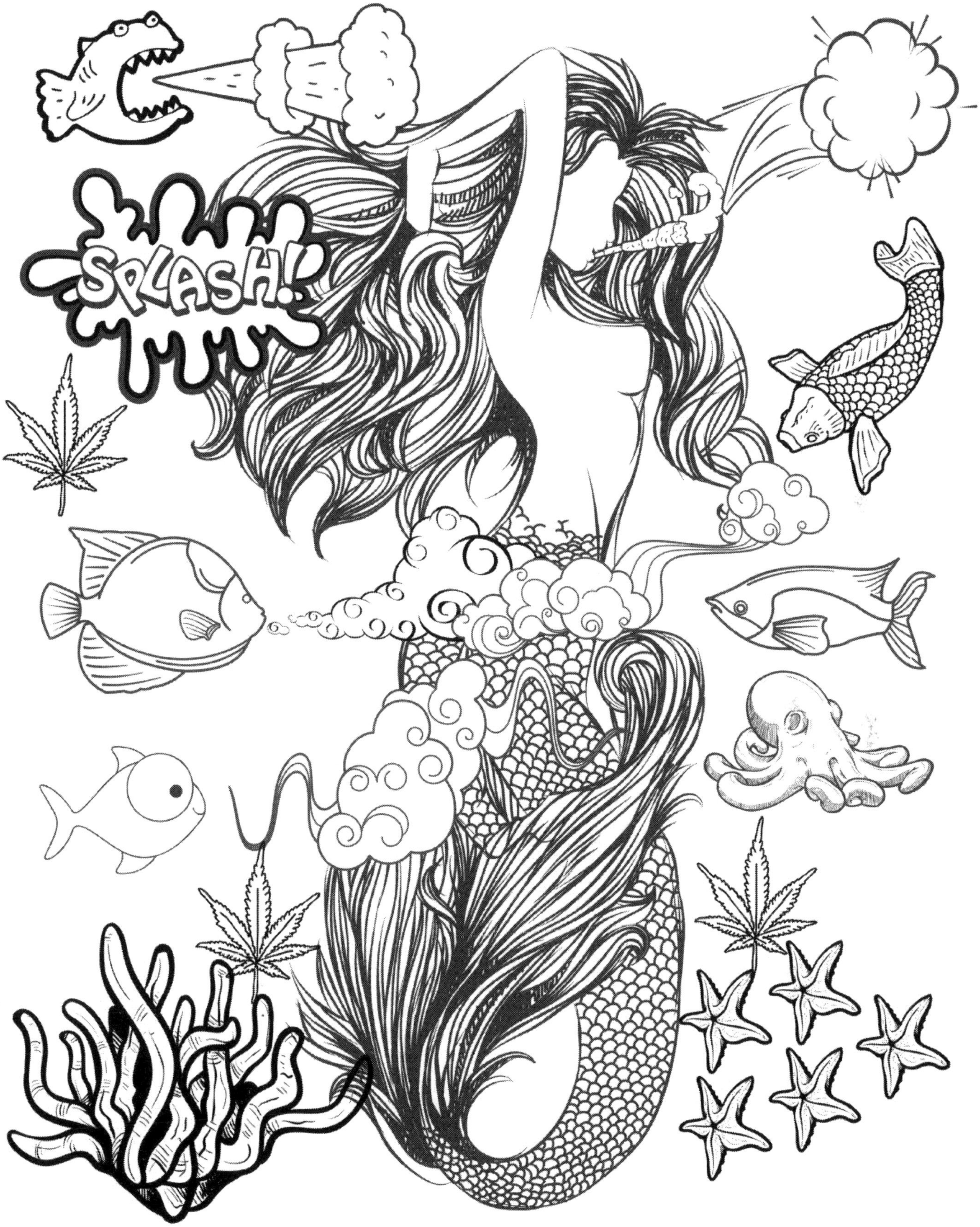
SPLASH!

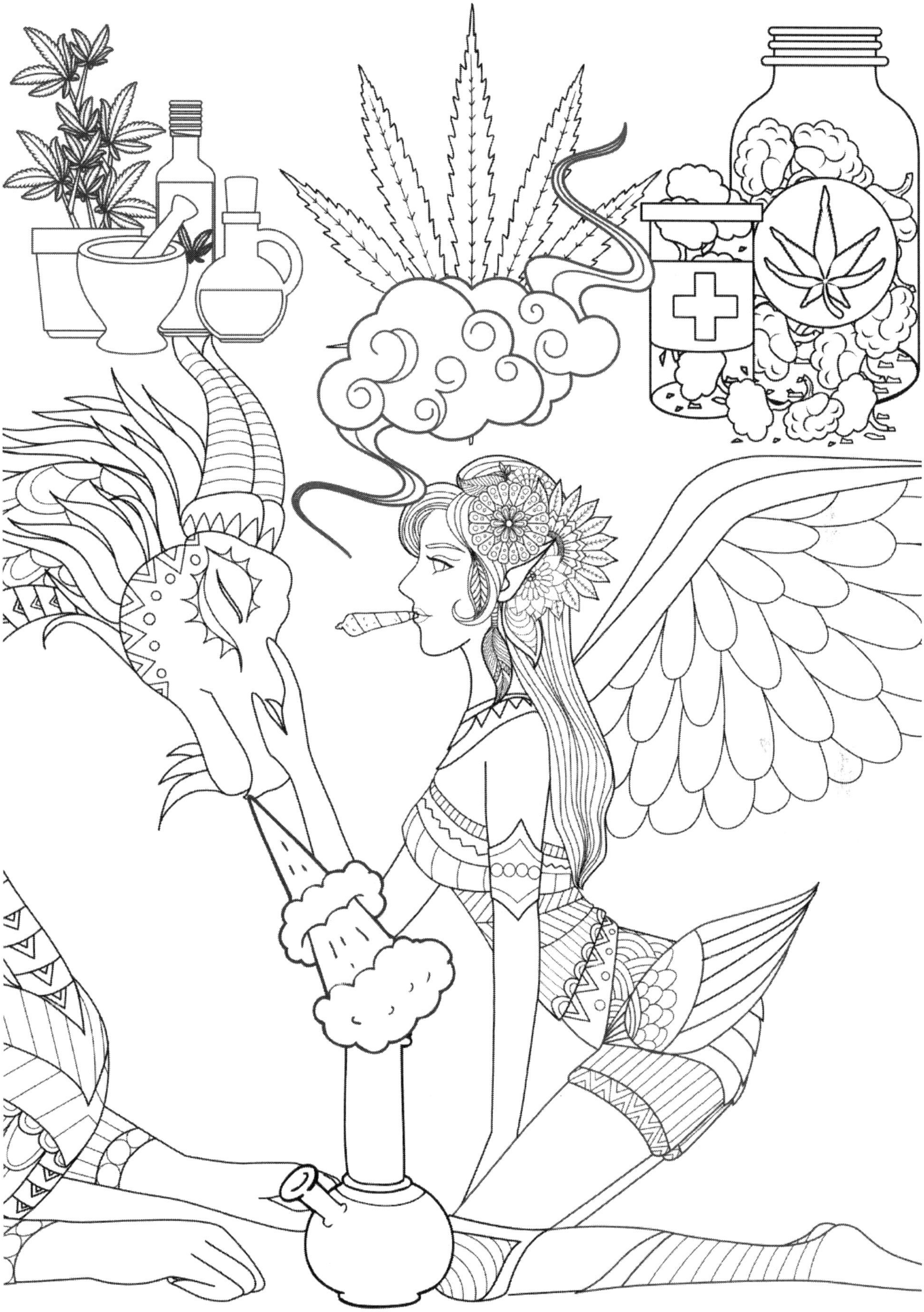

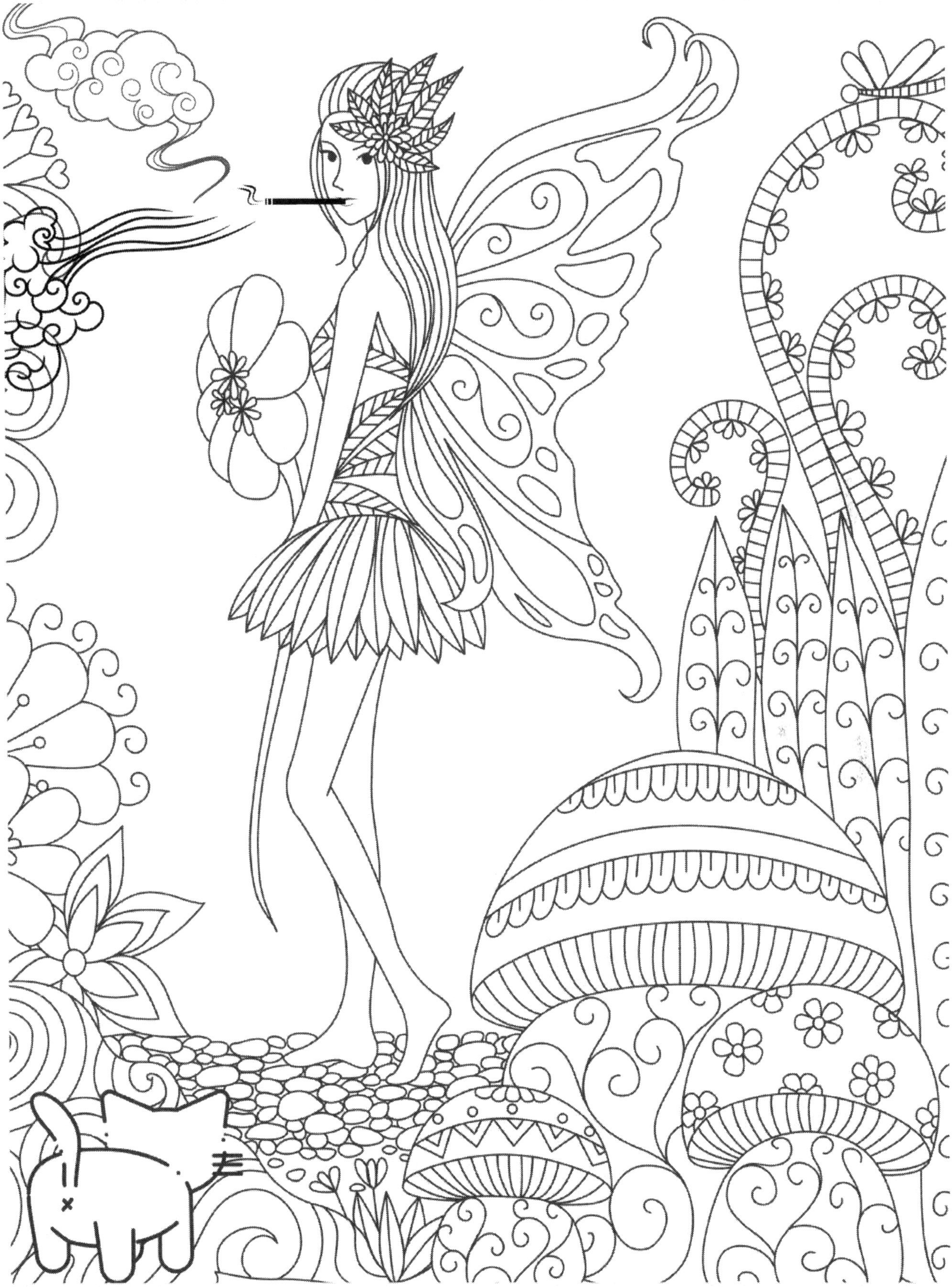

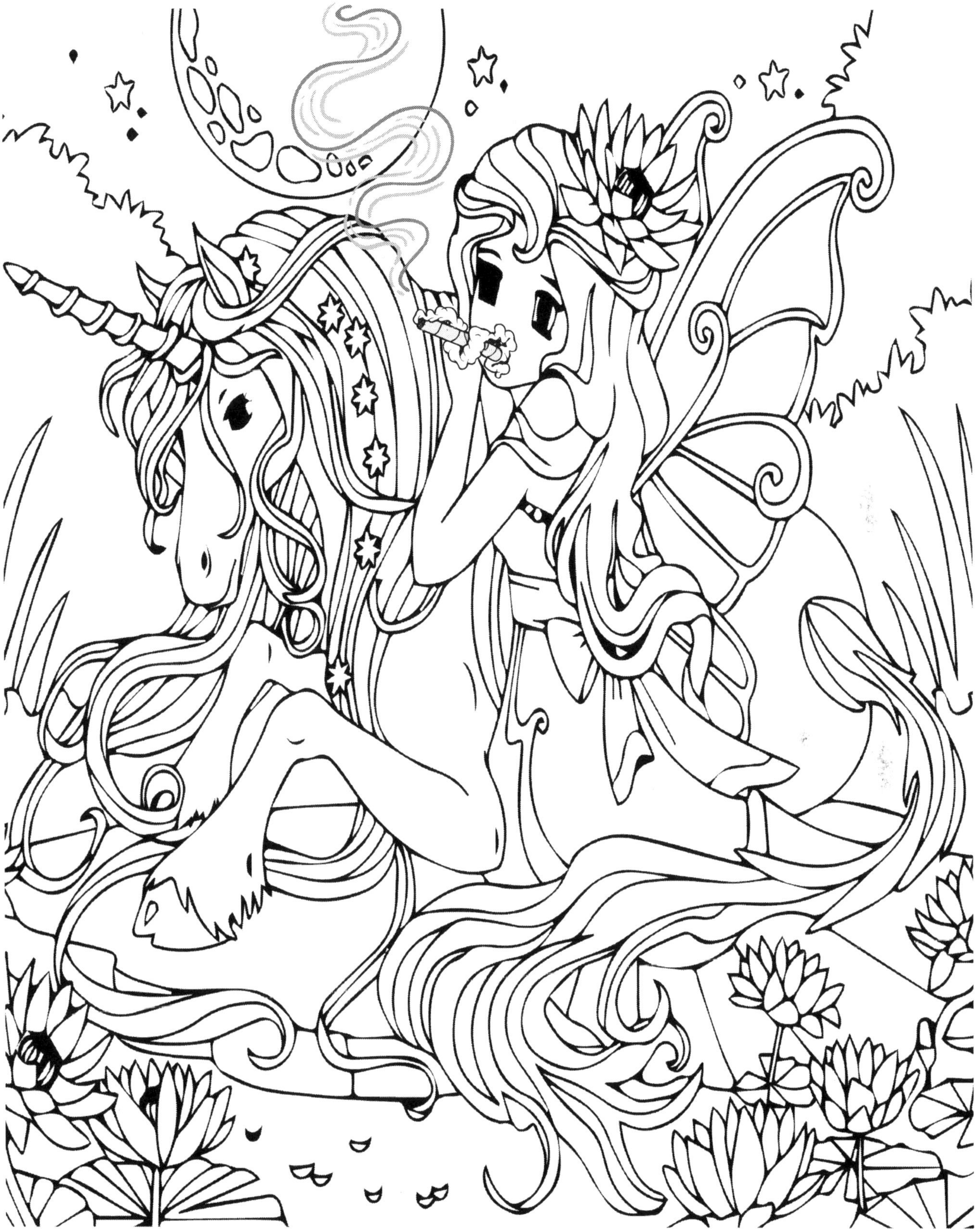

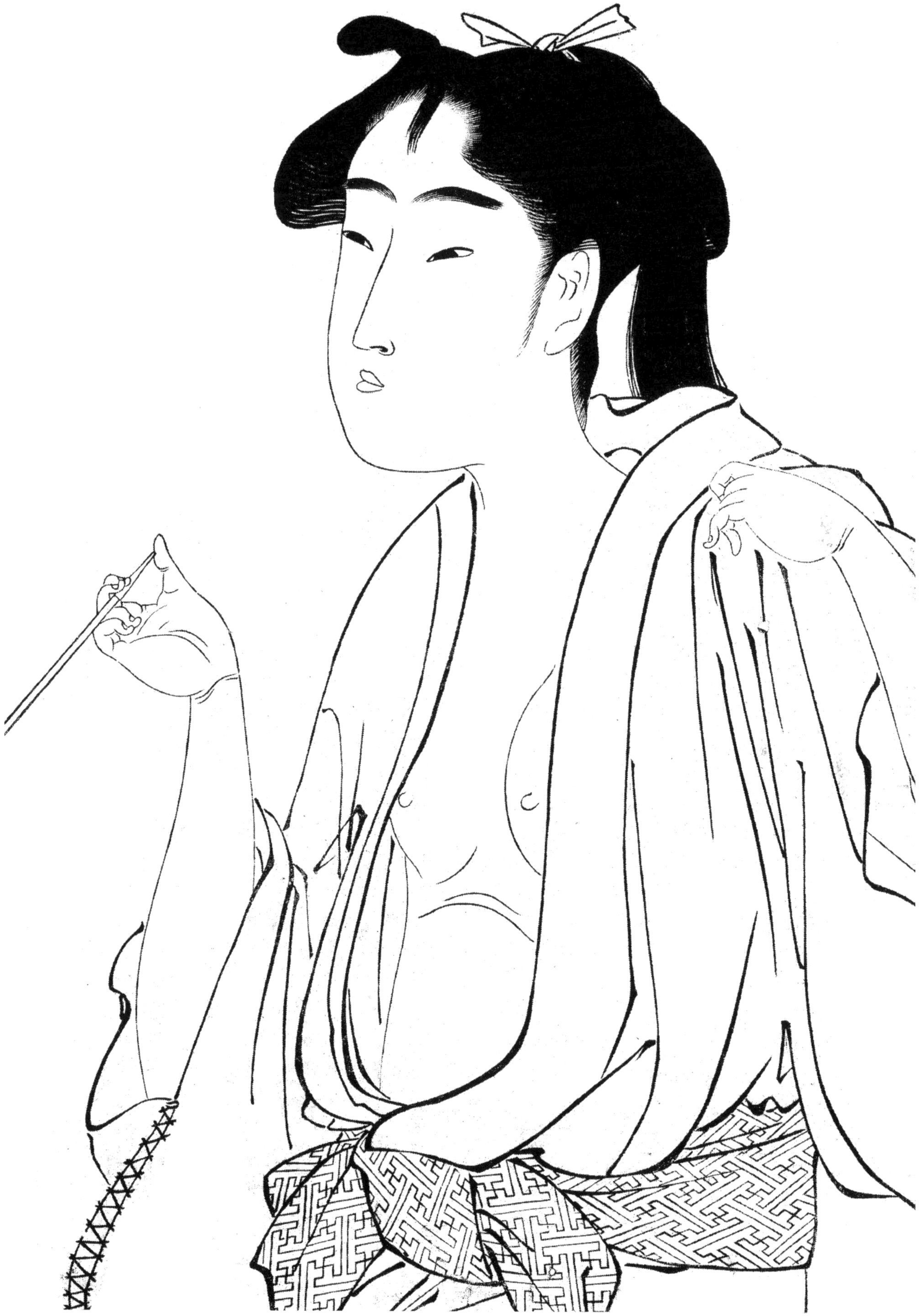

Thank you for your purchase,
if you like the product, please don't forget to give me a review on my amazon product page

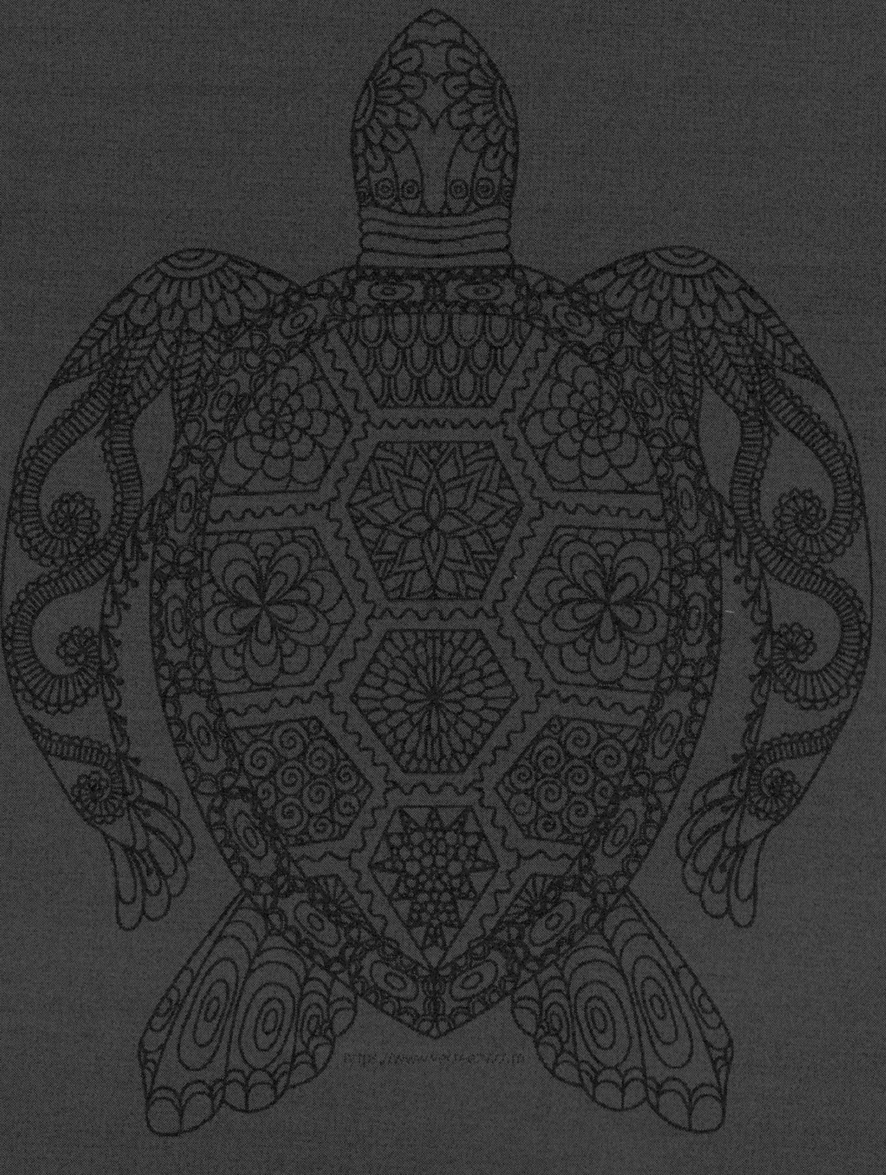